CW01512168

G
CENGAGE Learning

Psychologists and Their Theories for Students

Product Manager
Meggin Condino **Project Editor**
Kristine Krapp **Editorial**
Mark Springer

Indexing Services
Katherine Jensen **Rights and Aquisitions**
Margaret Abendroth, Ann Taylor **Imaging and Multimedia**
Robyn Young, Lezlie Light, Dan Newell **Product Design**
Pamela A. Galbreath **Manufacturing**
Evi Seoud, Lori Kessler © 2005, 2015 Gale, a part of Cengage Learning Inc.

For more information, contact
Gale, an imprint of Cengage Learning
27500 Drake Rd.
Farmington Hills, MI 48331-3535

Or you can visit our Internet site at
http://www.gale.com

LIBRARY OF CONGRESS CATALOGING-IN-PUBLICATION DATA

Psychologists and their theories for students / Kristine Krapp, editor.

 p. cm.

   Includes bibliographical references and index.
   ISBN 0-7876-6543-6 (set : hardcover : alk. paper) —
   ISBN 0-7876-6544-4 (v. 1) —
   ISBN 0-7876-6545-2 (v. 2)
   1. Psychologists. 2. Psychology.
   I. Krapp, Kristine M.

BF109.A1P72 2004

150'.92'2—dc22   2004011589

Printed in the United States of America 10 9 8 7 6 5
4 3 2 1

Wilhelm Max Wundt

1832–1920

GERMAN PSYCHOLOGIST, PROFESSOR

EXPERIMENTAL UNIVERSITY

UNIVERSITY OF HEIDELBERG, PhD, MD, 1856

BRIEF OVERVIEW

Wilhelm Max Wundt (1832–1920) opened an experimental laboratory that has been called the first of its kind in the history of psychology. By combining the methods of physiological examination with psychology theory, he created a whole new way to understand human behavior. Wundt has become known as the "founder of modern psychology," according to Thomas Hardy Leahey, author of the book *History of Psychology.* In 1987, Leahey wrote that Wundt "wedded physiology and psychology and made the resulting offspring independent." In 1875 Wundt was named a professor of physiology at the University of Leipzig, and he immediately established his innovative laboratory to empirically research his theories of psychology.

According to the 1997 *Biographical Dictionary of Psychology,* however, some of Wundt's colleagues disagreed with the designation of his laboratory's as the first of its kind. Two other experimental psychologists and contemporaries of Wundt, William James and G. Stanley Hall, both argued that they and others had employed similar experimentation methods in their labs. Yet Wundt did play a crucial role in the field as science was beginning to explore psychology in a new way. The dictionary comments that,

> the study of psychology had remained in the provinces of philosophy and the natural sciences. From philosophy had come (theories of) interactionsim, empiricism and materialism, theories hypothesizing the nature of the mind, mind–body interaction and acquisition of knowledge.

Wundt's early ideas were inspired by his colleague Johannes Müller's (1801–58) work in physiology. Müller used a system of specific procedures in his investigation of the human body that departed from the methods many others had used. Wundt had published his first book, *Grundzuge der physiologische Psychologie (Principles of Physiological Psychology)*, in 1873–74, setting forth the premise on which all of his work would be based. The book contained six volumes and was republished in several later editions, both during his lifetime and following his death. Wundt believed that the core of an organism's movement and motivations was a psychosocial process. In other words, the nature of any response in any organism, including humans, was a product of both physiological and psychological stimuli. His notion that mental occurrences could be objectively knowable and measurable became a fundamental principle that would trigger generations of psychological study and experimentation. Wundt was able to utilize the knowledge both of the sense organs and the control they exerted over the brain and consequently over control of movement. He used introspection as a tool for unlocking the human psyche. Wundt believed that no matter how complicated mental processes might seem, they could be broken down into a series of simple elements.

Wundt's fourth edition of his *Physiological Psychology*, published in 1893, presented his "tridimensional theory of feeling." Wundt thought that feelings could be classified as pleasant or unpleasant, tense or relaxed, or excited or depressed. Furthermore, any feeling could contain feelings from each of the three categories. His approach eventually came to be known as structuralism, a theory described by his student, E. B. Titchener. Structuralism "sought to describe the structure of consciousness, its basic building blocks, by carefully observing conscious experience," through the use of introspection.

Wundt's research findings laid the groundwork for psychologists for many generations. He was best recognized as having established psychology as a discipline independent of philosophy, incorporating elements of anatomy and physiology. He provided the scientific method to investigate the mind, which had long been believed to be unknowable. But even Wundt did not think that the scientific method could uncover answers to all of the questions in human psychology. "With particular reference to language and its development," one Wundt biographer wrote, "he sought understanding through the study of history and culture rather than through experimental analysis." Wundt would write extensively on those matters during the last years of his life. "His greatest strength was . . . the systematization and synthesis of work that had preceded him, thus preparing the foundation for experimental psychology."

BIOGRAPHY

Wilhelm Max Wundt was born on August 16, 1832, in Neckarau, a suburb of Mannheim, Germany. His father, Maximillian (1787–1846) was a Lutheran pastor whom Wundt once described as a "jovial and generous person, but generous to a fault." Wundt's mother, Maria Friederike Arnold Wundt, (1797–1868) was from a modestly wealthy family whose governess had taught her French as a child. When Wundt was four, his father accepted a position in Heidelsheim, a small country village in stark contrast to the bustling port of Mannheim. Being transferred to such a place indicated that the senior Wundt was not an ambitious man, and he showed few signs of promise or dynamic behavior.

Although Wundt did have siblings, he grew up as an only child. One sibling died before he was born, another he did not remember, and his brother Ludwig was sent at the age of ten to live with an aunt in Heidelberg when Wundt was only two years old. Ludwig died in 1902. Though he had many cousins, Wundt spent his Heidelsheim childhood without many peers, except at school. He was usually surrounded by adults, including some who were kind enough to pay attention to him and guide his interests. A student of the village school for only two years, Wundt was prepared for a more disciplined academic career by his father's assistant pastor, Friedrich Müller, who tutored him until he was sent to boarding school at the age of 13.

Müller's time spent in hours of study brought him closer to Wundt than the boy was to his own father and mother. As a child, Wundt's only real friend was a boy described as "mentally retarded with defective speech" who waited daily for him at the Wundt's cottage door. He became anxious when playing with other boys his own age, usually preferring to avoid the experience. Instead, he read voraciously from his father's library. Even before Wundt could write himself, he took on a literary project of compiling a history of what was common in all religions—aided in part not only through his experience of being the pastor's son, but by his experiences visiting a local Jewish merchant family and observing their prayer rituals in the synagogue and in their home. He was just 10 years old when he first read Shakespeare, and that pastime remained one of his pleasures throughout his life. With so much time spent alone, he also became a daydreamer whose studied introspection would lead him into the course of his professional life as a psychologist.

Wundt spoke little of his father or his paternal relatives. Wundt's daughter would later note that his paternal grandfather was pastor of a church at Wieblingen, a small town near Heidelberg where he had been also been a professor at the university, teaching about Baden's history and geography. Wundt's father had entered the life of the ministry not by choice, but because he was forced to replace the spot that had been originally held for his older brother, who had abandoned the study of theology. The family's long history in the pastoral life was important enough for Maximillian to take his place in it as well. A great-grandfather and two great uncles had also been members of the university faculty; these predecessors represented an honored status of academic and professional achievement which Wundt's father could never quite reach. Wundt recalled that his mother took the active role in managing the family's meager finances and attending to her son's education. He also remembered receiving loving consolation from his father after having been disciplined by his mother.

Wundt opened his autobiography with two exceptions to his fond memories about his father. "The first was a traumatic tumble down a flight of cellar stairs, and its recall was always accompanied by a vague feeling that this had happened while he was attempting to follow his father into the cellar," a Wundt biographer related. "In the other, Wundt was roused from a classroom reverie by a blow on the ear and looked up to see his father glowering over him." That particular day, his father's pastoral duties had included the role of school inspector—a person assigned to monitor the students in order to maintain discipline and to make sure that the classroom was being run properly—and the elder Wundt had observed his son misbehaving. The perception of his father as someone other than the loving person he thought he knew probably influenced Wundt negatively. Seeing his father as a source of pain might have led the young Wundt, who had identified so wholly with his father, to distrust himself.

Wundt also recalled two other public events that had had a great impact on him. The first memory was described by his biographer as follows,

> In Heidelsheim, on the afternoon of the final day of his first year's schooling, he watched from his doorstep as a crowd of peasants erected a "freedom tree" in the public square. Then he saw the burgomaster's house set ablaze by the demonstrators and later—while the local bailiff paced up and down inside the Wundt cottage—he saw them dispersed by a squadron of dragoons (soldiers armed with short muskets for the purpose of persecution).

PRINCIPAL PUBLICATIONS

- *Principles   of   Physiological*

Psychology. 1873–74. Reprint, Engleman, 1911.

- *Outlines of Psychology.* Translated by C.H. Judd., 1896. Reprint, Engleman, 1907.

- *Volkerpsychologie (Elements of Folk Psychology).* 10 vols, Engleman, 1900–1920.

- *Lectures on Human and Animal Psychology.* Translated by J.E. Crighton and E.B. Titchener. Macmillan, 1984.

When Wundt was not yet 17, three years after his father's death, the Republic of Baden was established. In June, Wundt witnessed the flashes of cannon fire in the distance, as Prussian army troops set out to suppress the young republic's independence. During the 1860s, Wundt became actively involved in the Workers' Educational League and served as a member of the Baden diet, or governing body, probably due to the influence of these experiences.

Upon his father's death, his maternal uncles assumed a prominent role in Wundt's education. His mother's two brothers, Johann Wilhelm and Philipp Friedrich, had both studied medicine at Heidelberg, and they had also begun to teach at the university. His uncle Friedrich had an especially illustrative career as an anatomy and physiology professor, and his influence secured Wundt a position at Heidelberg in 1858.

Formal schooling and the university

A year before he left for boarding school, Müller received his own pastorate in Münzesheim, not very far from Heidelsheim. Wundt was not happy with the situation, and eventually his parents let him move in with the younger pastor in order to continue his studies. When he entered the Bruchsal gymnasium (a college preparatory school), Wundt was sent to live with another Lutheran pastor's family there in what was a predominately Catholic town. That year turned out to be a disaster for him. He performed poorly at school, was homesick, and was unable to make friends. Once he even ran away back to his home. His mother took him back to school, however, as she was determined that he should get a proper education. At the end of the year, one of his teachers suggested to his parents that perhaps he could pursue a career in the postal service, since it was clear that he was probably not cut out for a profession that required any serious academic excellence.

His mother and her relatives ignored this advice and decided that young Wilhelm deserved a second chance. He was sent to his aunt's home in Heidelberg to join his brother Ludwig, who had become a very studious young man and a student at the university. His aunt enrolled Wundt in the

Heidelberg gymnasium, where he experienced a whole new life of making friends and becoming active in extracurricular activities. His studies remained average rather than outstanding—a fact that one biographer suggested may have been due to his consuming interest in politics, especially the struggle for Baden's independence and the uprising of the Polish peasants in Heidelsheim. Following his father's death at the end of his first year in Heidelberg, some historians have suggested that his mother went to live in Heidelberg, too. If so, it is likely that Wundt moved in with his mother, and continued to live with her during the early years of his academic career. Once he became old enough attend college, Wundt was relieved that his mediocre grades were high enough to obtain financial aid from the state to attend the University of Heidelberg. As a young man who had been so close to his family, he was ready to venture out on his own, at least for a while. Because his mother's younger brother Friedrich was a professor at Tübingen, Wundt was able to persuade his mother to allow him to attend that school. His uncle's influence transformed Wundt into a serious student who developed a passion for the study of cerebral anatomy. By that time, as well, Friedrich Arnold had accepted the position as the director of Heidelberg's Anatomical Institute, and the logical course for Wundt would have been to follow him back to Heidelberg, now that he had proven himself in his studies.

Wundt certainly was serious about his studies in a way he had not been before. But he needed to make up many courses in mathematics and science that he had neglected while a gymnasium student. As a result, he studied mathematics with a private tutor while completing lecture and laboratory courses in physics and chemistry. A newly arrived professor of chemistry, Robert Bunsen (after whom the Bunsen burner was named) had Wundt so enthused about the subject that for a brief time he considered changing his major to chemistry instead of working toward a medical degree. He stayed with medicine, however, and in 1855 Wundt successfully passed his state exams, becoming a licensed doctor. Even more remarkably, this once-marginal student earned the highest scores on every separate test: internal medicine, surgery, and obstetrics.

Professional career

Wundt had passed his medical examinations and received his medical degree. That feat alone far surpassed his and his family's expectations. Still, he was not completely convinced of his ability to sustain a regular medical practice. His inclination was to perform something of social consequence in his work. He did not become a doctor in order to serve only the wealthy people who could afford his professional services. Wundt had even considered becoming a military physician—an option that turned out to be unavailable during that period of peace when no such openings existed. When a friend who was working at a local city hospital needed to take six months away to study for his medical exams, he offfered Wundt the temporary post. Relieved to have such a post available to him, Wundt accepted. The hospital job presented many challenges. He was responsible for treating women in the public ward, and many of his patients were peasants, servants, and prostitutes. He was often on call for 24 hours at a time.

Two incidents during his tenure at the hospital helped Wundt decide that he was better suited for an academic career. Once, when he had been awakened from a deep sleep, Wundt mistakenly administered iodine to a patient in need of a narcotic for pain. Even after the alert patient spit the iodine out into his face, Wundt did not fully awake. Thoughts about that near-catastrophe haunted him the rest of his life; in the short term, the error made him seriously question his medical abilities. The other problem was described by a biographer, who noted that the hospital often treated paralyzed patients who had suffered leg injuries and other accidents.

> In checking on the course of recovery, Wundt made fairly systematic observations on the impairment of localization of touch sensations, and he came to the conclusion that the results could not be harmonized with Weber's theory (E. H. Weber, 1846) that localization is based on a mosaic organization of the sensory innervation of the skin.

Wundt concluded that sensation alterations in these patients had not only physiological, but also psychological, implications. That experience marked his first foray into considering psychological issues, and he knew he would not be satisfied unless he pursued the matter. Without the support of his family, Wundt managed to gather enough money to attend a semester in Berlin where he studied simultaneously under Johannes Müller and Emil Du Bois-Reymond. Müller's *Handbook of Human Physiology,* published in 1833–1840, had already captured its place in history as the standard text that recognized physiology as a science. Du Bois-Reymond's 1848 book, *Researches on Animal Electricity,* had established him as the expert in electrophysiology.

Wundt returned to Heidelberg in the spring of 1857. He became an instructor there, teaching a general survey of experimental physiology in his first semester. Shortly into his teaching career, however, Wundt became seriously ill. Without warning, he began to hemorrhage violently. What the doctors thought about his potential for recovery had no influence on him. He himself believed he was near death. Wundt related the story by saying that it had brought him a "perfect tranquillity," giving him an entirely different perspective on his life. A biographer observed:

> Whether or not these attitudes were ultimately traceable to this traumatic experience, as Wundt implied, they were characteristic of much of Wundt's later work, and the reader must therefore be prepared to accept the fact that Wundt's

empiricism, except in his earliest period, had mystical as well as experimental aspects.

Wundt stayed at Heidelberg until 1874. During his tenure there, he was promoted from the position of instructor to associate professor. In 1858, the noted physiologist, physicist, and psychologist Hermann von Helmholtz arrived at the university; shortly thereafter, Wundt began to serve as his assistant. His major projects at Heidelberg included the study of the neurological and chemical stimulation of muscles. Wundt's first writings, *Beiträge zur Theorie der Sinneswahrenehmungen,* were published in installments between 1858 and 1862, and also in a combined edition in 1862. This book contained much of his teaching, along with an overview of the work he would continue to pursue throughout his career. In the 1984 *Biographical Dictionary of Psychology,* the author stated, "In his work, Wundt made the point that psychology, before tackling metaphysical problems, should start by trying to understand the simplest experiences, and that this should be done using the methods of physiology." His most significant publication, *Grundzuge der physiologischen Psychologie, (The Principles of Physiological Psychology)* first appeared in 1873. The sixth, and last, revision of the work was completed in 1911.

At the age of 40, Wundt had still not received significant professional recognition; he remained an associate professor at Heidelberg. Although he had been recommended for an opening at Zurich

University, possibly as early as 1872 when the chair of inductive philosophy was made vacant, he was not formally offered the position until the following year. Wundt delivered a memorable inaugural address when he arrived, offering himself as the philosopher who had come to fill the appropriate chair. He mentioned the names of other notable philosophers—including Aristotle, Gottfried Wilhelm von Leibniz, John Locke, Georg Wilhelm Hegel, and Immanuel Kant. Wundt had finally begun to gain some notoriety. The academic world of physiology and psychology was finally beginning to listen to him.

Leipzig

After a short tenure at Zurich, Wundt accepted the chair of philosophy at the University of Leipzig in 1875. He would stay in Leipzig for the rest of his life. In his inaugural message there in 1876, Wundt said that:

> The more we are inclined today, and rightly, to demand that experience shall have an influence on philosophy, so much the more is it in place to emphasize that precisely in our time philosophy must assert its old influence among the empirical sciences . . . Nothing can be more mistaken than the widespread opinion that these [empirical and materialistic] views emerged from the development of natural science itself. The

standpoint of modern empiricism got its foundation from philosophers . . . Perhaps the time will not be far distant when the metaphysics which is now so scorned by empirical investigators will again be held in some measure of honor.

Soon after he was settled in Leipzig, Wundt set up his first room for demonstrations in the field of research that would come to be known as sensation and perception. An American psychologist named William James, who had also studied under Helmholtz and would remain at odds with Wundt's approach, set up a similar lab the same year at Harvard. By 1879, with his experimental laboratory fully established, Wundt would mentor his first American graduate assistant, G. Stanley Hall, and a whole new era would begin in the study of psychology (see accompanying sidebar).

BIOGRAPHY:
G. Stanley Hall

G. Stanley Hall (1844–1924) was a young teacher at Antioch College in Yellow Springs, Ohio, during the early 1870s when he first read Wundt's *Principles of Physiological Psychology*. As a student of both Wundt and Helmholtz, and later as a friend to William James, Hall received the first Ph.D. in psychology to be granted in the United States. Although he became known as much for his work in education as he was known for psychology, he remained devoted to both. He also followed in the footsteps on Wundt and James, establishing experimental labs at Johns Hopkins University in Maryland in 1883, which was second only to James' lab in America, and at Clark University in Massachusetts in 1889.

Granville Stanley Hall was born on February 1, 1844, in the small farming town of Ashfield, Massachusetts. He was the son of Granville Bascom and Abigail Beals Hall. When Hall graduated from Williams College in 1867, he went to the Union Theological Seminary in New York City. A grant of $500 the following year gave him the means to travel to Bonn and Berlin, where he studied theology and philosophy. From 1871 until 1876, he taught at Antioch before moving on to Harvard to complete his Ph.D. on the muscular perception of space. When he returned to Germany to study with the famous physiologists Wundt and Helmholtz, he gathered enough knowledge to pursue his own path in psychology.

Hall joined the faculty at Johns

Hopkins, where in 1883 he established his own laboratory. His facility was regarded as the first working psychology lab in the United States—James's lab at Harvard was considered a teaching laboratory. In 1887 he began to publish the *American Journal of Psychology*. Hall founded other journals as well, including the *Pedagogical Seminary,* known currently as the *Journal of Genetic Psychology,* 1891; the *Journal of Applied Psychology,* 1915; and, the *Journal of Religious Psychology,* which he published between 1904 and 1914. One of his most impressive acts was founding the American Psychological Association on July 8, 1892, when he invited 26 of the world's leading psychologists to attend a meeting. Only James and Dewey were unable to attend. By the end of the twentieth century, more than half of the world's psychologists belonged to the association.

As a pioneer in developmental psychology, also known as genetic psychology, Hall had been influenced by British naturalist Charles Darwin and his theory of evolution. Hall consequently began to reflect on childhood development, and he played a key role in the child study movement that grew for years in the United States. The movement did not last in that form, but it did provide the basis for the idea that studying children was beneficial and established the need for empirical work in that field. In 1909, Hall invited the famous psychologists Sigmund Freud and Carl Jung to lecture at the school. At the time of this conference, even the professional community regarded the field with suspicion. Hall was the pioneer who introduced psychoanalysis to America.

His interest in the psychology of religion led Hall to publish *Jesus, the Christ, in the Light of Psychology,* in 1917. His other major works included, *Adolescence: Its Psychology and its Relations to Physiology, Anthropology, Sociology, Sex, Crime, Religion and Education,* published in 1904; and *Life and Confessions of a Psychologist,* in 1923.

Hall was married to Cornelia Fisher in September 1879; and to Florence E. Smith, in July 1899. He had two children. He died on April 24, 1924, in Worcester, Massachusetts.

Students and psychologists from all over the world worked in Wundt's lab and eventually returned to their home countries to set up their own. A movement had begun that continues today. By the winter term of 1883–84, Wundt's laboratory had gained official status as an institute of the Department of Philosophy at Leipzig. Among his other contributions to his profession, Wundt founded the journal, *Philosophische Studien,* as a publication venue for the results of his experiments and those of his students. In 1903 the name of the journal was changed to *Psychologische Studien,* reflecting the new climate of acceptance for the serious scientific study of psychology.

In addition to his methodical research methods, Wundt was known for his quiet demeanor and diligence. When lecturing, for example, he could go on for more than two hours without using notes or pausing for questions. During the school year of 1889–90, he was elected to the post of vice-chancellor of the university, and in 1902 he was made an honorary citizen of Leipzig. In 1915 he was named a professor emeritus. Social and cultural psychology eventually occupied much of Wundt's time and study in his later years. He did not believe that his experimental methods were applicable to most areas of psychology. This shift in direction returned him to his first loves of literature, arts, and the ritualistic practices common among various ethnic and cultural groups that he believed revealed the true essence of cultural psychology. He published his 10-volume series, *Volkerpsychologie (Folk Psychology),* between 1900 and 1920.

Wundt married Sophie Mau in 1872. The couple had one daughter, Eleonore, who served as her father's personal secretary and assistant. She continued to preside over his work even after his death, and she also provided assistance to scholars who were studying her father's work. She was important enough, in fact, that when Chiba Tanenari, the first chair of psychology at Tokoku Imperial University, began to purchase the Wundt collection, he visited with Eleonore in Groábothen, the small town near Leipzig where the Wundts had made their home. Most of Wundt's personal collection remains in Japan today, due to the skillful negotiations and financing of Tanenari and his Japanese colleagues, who respected Wundt's work immensely and had elevated him to an enormous stature.

Wundt finished writing his autobiography, *Erlebtes and Erkanntes,* in 1920, not long before he died. In death as in life, Wundt would continue to have his disciples as well as his detractors. James had said that he was "only a rather ordinary man who has worked up certain things uncommonly well." Biographers Rieber and Robinson offered their own perspective on the importance of studying Wundt nearly a hundred years after his death.

> The contributors to this collection do not pretend to cover every aspect of the vast work and complex influence of Wundt on psychology. We also do not speak with one voice. In fact, if you do not find argument and provocation in these pages, then we have failed in our task. Early experimental psychology was a complex enterprise, and the difficulties in interpreting and understanding it do not seem to lessen over time. So we agree on many things, disagree on quite a few things, and discuss all our ideas and readings in a spirit not only of mutual respect, but of outright enthusiasm and

love for the productive argument.

THEORIES

The titles and headings that Wundt used in his work were as much a part of understanding his work as the theories themselves. In the case of his *Principles of Physiological Psychology,* (1902 edition) the categories he provided served as more than simply an outline. They provided a direction, resonating with the significance of organization that Wundt brought to psychology: Part I, "The Bodily Substrate of the Mental Life;" Chapter I, "The Organic Evolution of Mental Function;" and, Section 1, "The Criteria of Mind and the Range of the Mental Life." His first paragraph for that edition presented the guiding force, not only for this treatise, but for his entire, lifelong investigation. He wrote that:

> The mental functions form a part of the phenomena of life. Wherever we observe them, they are accompanied by the processes of nutrition and reproduction. On the other hand, the general phenomena of life may be manifested in cases where we have no reason for supposing the presence of mind. Hence the first question that arises, is an inquiry concerning the bodily substrate [defined here as the foundation, or core element upon which a force acts to cause change or motion] of mentality, is this: What are

the characteristics that justify our attributing mental functions to a living body, an object in the domain of animate nature?

Wundt was not the first scientist to begin such an investigation, and he conducted his research at a time when the destination of such an inquiry remained unknown. He was like an engineer who tears down a building that he has analyzed from its pinnacle, examining each piece of the demolished structure to see how the whole had been created from the parts. In the case of human beings and the state of their mental life, Wundt began with the top of the pyramid—the human—and worked his way down to the smallest organism capable of sustaining life. His stated his mission this way:

> Here, upon the very threshold of physiological psychology, we are confronted with unusual difficulties. The distinguishing characteristics of mind are of a subjective sort; we know them only from the contents of our own consciousness. But the question calls for objective criteria, from which we shall be able to argue to the presence of a consciousness. Now the only possible criteria of the kind consist in certain bodily movements, which carry with them an indication of their origin in psychical processes.

According to one biographical profile, Wundt's

fame was "based principally on his having founded an experimental psychological science." Many critics and historians have suggested that his views and research were not as important as the methods he established for psychological investigation. Even Helmholtz declared that Wundt's experiments were "sloppy," and not up to his standards. The question remains whether Wundt has been represented fairly by observers and critics throughout history.

Wundt's basic tool of introspection became the guiding force for his research as well as for others' investigations. His ultimate goal was to understand human consciousness and the mental processes that composed the elements of it. His underlying approach to testing would later become known as structuralism, particularly under the American interpretation of Wundt's methods.

Main points

In theory, Wundt believed that the complexity of the human mental experience could be broken down into three main types: sensations, images, and feelings.

Sensations As Wundt explained them, sensations were the basic forms of experience. They consisted of a direct relationship between an excitation, or stimulus, of the cerebral cortex (a center of intellectual functioning in the brain) and a sensory experience. These sensations could be placed into categories including modality, vision, or audition, in addition to describing such features as intensity and duration.

Images Images were basically the same concept as sensations, though these were associated with a local stimulus in the cortex rather than an external stimulus outside the body.

Feelings The category of feelings represented whatever did not come from the sense organs or a "revival of sensory experience." The "tridimensional theory of feeling" was Wundt's premise that all feelings could be categorized by three different sets of opposing emotions—pleasant or unpleasant, tense or relaxed, and excited or depressed. Any combination of one of each of the sets could describe any feeling.

General principles of the central functions

In the 1902 edition of Principles of Physiological Psychology, Wundt focused on the central functions, or the central nervous system. In discussing the research and experimentation that led to his conclusions, Wundt presented what he termed, "General principles of the central functions."

The five general principles that Wundt explained were:

- the principle of connection of elements
- the principle of original indifference of functions

- the principle of practice and adaptation
- the principle of vicarious function
- the principle of relative localization

Principle of connection of elements

Explanation Wundt classified his approach to understanding the nervous system in three different ways: anatomical, physiological, and psychological. In terms of anatomy, the system was made up of many elements that were closely connected to one another. The nerve cells, or neurons, were controlled by the cell processes. The results of the cell processes often provided clues as to the directions in which the connections are made, Wundt noted. This principle also indicated that every physiological activity was also the sum of many functions, even if the researcher is unable to separate those functions from the whole and from the organism's complex behavior. Again, as with the other two perspectives, Wundt's described "physical" or psychological contents indicated that each of the complicated nerve processes can be broken down into its basic elements, all of which react in cooperation to create the whole. The indicators of this structure are found in the process of psychological observation itself, Wundt noted, and the fact that any psychical process imaginable —no matter how simple—must have arisen from a large group of interconnected pieces, or elements.

Examples As an example of the anatomical sense of the connection element, Wundt offered that "the merit of the 'neurone theory' to have shown how this principle of the connection of elements is exhibited in the morphological relations of the central nervous system." The example that he used for the physiological aspect was that every sensation or muscular contraction are really complex processes that can be analyzed as the activities of a lot of different parts—the act of standing up out of a chair, for instance, is not one movement, but the result of many different steps that produce the result of standing. In the psychological view, Wundt noted that the "arousal of light or tone," is not simply the "action of stimulus upon the peripheral structures, but also and invariably the processes of nervous conduction, the excitations of central elements in the mesencephalic region, and finally certain processes in the cortical centers." As in the case of memory images, Wundt explained, it is the coordination center that is first involved in the activity, and subsequently the peripheral region.

Principle of original indifference of functions

Explanation Just as he theorized that the structure of functions could be broken down into their elements, Wundt outlined all of these five principles with the same understanding. Based on the "connection of elements," Wundt determined that the hypothesis of "wherever the physiological functions of the central elements have acquired a specific coloring (or peculiar quality) this unique character does not come from the elements themselves but rather from the connections." He offered evidence that this functional indifference had long been the norm by pointing out two phenomena existed to show that it was true. First, he stated that the function of the peripheral organs must represent a lengthy, continuous pattern in order for the sensations to appear in a person's consciousness. And, second, the disturbances of the function caused by central lesions could be "compensated [for] without disappearance of the lesions themselves."

Examples Wundt's premise in support of the first phenomena was that people born blind or deaf, or who have lost those senses in early childhood, did not have the sensations of light or sound. He concluded that the complex interaction and relation of the sensory aspects that are part of the "higher mental processes," meaning those more advanced, or complex, were a part of a central nervous system that was comprised, not of the origin of new specific qualities, but rather of the "indefinitely" complex interrelation of specific sensory elements of the mind.

Principle of practice and adaptation

Explanation Wundt used the word "practice" in the standard meaning of the term—as in the repeated performance of a function. With regard to the nervous system, practice indicated that every key element would get better as it went through the ongoing process of being fitted to perform or participate in a particular function. Adaptation would come with the practice and it would cause changes along the way until a different combination was born.

Examples When adaptation occurred with regard to nervous functions, the resulting adaptations that would become most important are those "newly practiced" elements which would take the place of the older ones.

Principle of vicarious function

Explanation Following directly from the previous principle, "vicarious function" was a special case of practice and adaptation: namely, one with a limited prospect. In other words, it involved a new structural extension that would be required to perform a function new to the involved elements. The structure has an inherent capability to perform the new task, even though it has never been expressed before. This idea can be broken down into two forms—a substitution by "extension of the area of function" and a substitution that happens by acquiring new functions. The first substitution was a gradual "compensation" of the disturbances. This occurred as a result of a significant partial impairment due to the increased activity in other areas that also shared in the function. Sometimes these compensations would come from the "higher" centers, and thus wipe out the trouble that was caused by the lesions of the "lower" centers.

Examples In the first form of substitution, Wundt used the example of what happened in certain cases of brain injury that are centered in the cerebellum or in the diencephalic and mesencephalic regions (part of the forward part and the middle part) of the brain —at least, as much as he knew in the latter part of the nineteenth century. He noted that the disturbances will gradually disappear in these cases of injury. The forms of vicarious function that involved spatial connection were different, according to Wundt. This difference could be understood by imagining that the speech centers of the brain just do not work. That they did not become atrophied could be a difficult concept to figure out, were it not for a simple explanation: If every complex function was based on the supposition that the central elements cooperate in a very detailed and complex manner, then the evidence suggested that more than just one area was involved in such a function. If aphasia—the loss of the ability to use or understand language that often accompanies an injury such as a stroke—occurred when the centers for speech in the left side of the brain were destroyed, the conclusion that these speech functions were solely based in that left side of the brain would be incorrect. Again, in this case, Wundt believed that speech was a cooperative function, with some language processing based in the right side of the brain, even if it was the smaller part of the function. Even though one side of the brain might be used more heavily in a certain task, that side was not the only method the brain used.

Because of that statement, substitution by using the functions of the other side was possible.

Principle of relative localization

Explanation Wundt argued that even though the central functions and peripheral organs had their own distinct places, the central organ provided a way that those functions could join together. Titchener's translation of this text said that, "any absolute localization of function" was impossible. Yet, considering the fact that the central location of a system was not fixed, the movements of the various functions would have to be relative to environmental conditions, both internal and external. Concluding his discussion of this concept, Wundt explained that this principle included all of the preceding principles, and that therefore the idea of absolute localization contradicted all of them.

Examples Wundt offered as an example of relative localization the understanding that a reference to the "visual center" was not restricted to the visual cortex; rather, nerve centers outside the brain also played an important role in the function of vision.

Summary of the central function principles

These five principles, Wundt noted, were not easily accepted with regard to the development of the central functions theory. Many other researchers had opposing views. Wundt's defense of his principles failed to dismiss that opposition. "Their progress was hindered, from the outset," Wundt wrote, "by the authority of scientific tradition; in some measure, more particularly in the domain of anatomical and physiological research." This body of the argument of Wundt's five principles offered a differing viewpoint, and in some cases, antagonistic, of previously held ideas about nerve physiology. Wundt did not intend for this theory, or any other of his theories, to be the final word, however. He simply wanted to foster continued experimentation and exploration that was based in sound scientific judgment.

Main points: Other key principles

Other theories grew out of Wundt's basic premise of critical introspection. These principles not only guided Wundt in his research, but they also provided Wundt's students and critics with numerous premises to examine. Five different key approaches emerged as the foundations of his thought.

Actuality principle

Wundt believed in the notion of consciousness as a natural reality. In order to track his system, the student of his work must also accept that premise—but methods of studying subjective experience were problematic. Wundt understood the immense challenge of such a task. As he reviewed the trials of his own personal life and growth, however, he believed it could be solved. One biographer noted:

> Wundt placed his subject matter in line to be another level following upwards in the series of sciences, *physics, chemistry, and biology.* Differences of considerable substance, however, separate this next level from the others. Physical sciences are about objects and energies conceptualized by physical scientists. Consciousness is not a thing–like physical concept. Rather, it is an immediate and transient *process,* the investigation of which amounts to no less than the study of *subjectivity.* Consciousness is a continuous flow, a constant unfolding of experience, which according to Wundt's findings cannot be separated into discrete "faculties" as had been done in ancient times.

This argument comprised Wundt's principle of actuality.

Explanation Wundt and his researchers determined that consciousness worked in a unique way, and they believed that the elements of that operation could be observed and described. That belief alone provided motivation to push forward in defining the new science of psychology. Included in their discoveries were verifiable limitations of "mental capacities, on span, on the timing of the temporal flow, on the nature of selective attention and short-term memory," as a biographer stated. They found a limited number, usually six or seven, "attentional fixations" that resulted from each timing measure through which short-term memories were stored. Any differences among those experiences of sensation and emotion revealed a multidimensional aspect. Behaviors were thus motivated by the urges and tensions that had resulted from these combined experiences. The observation of these phenomena also revealed how these behaviors might fluctuate, which ones resulted from self-control, which took effort to manipulate, and which were automatically performed, similar to natural reflexes.

Examples Emil Kraepelin, a student of Wundt's, proposed a theory of schizophrenia in 1917. It was based largely on what was beginning to emerge as Wundt's theoretical system. Kraepelin utilized Wundt's details of what has been described as "processes of central selective attention." Kraepelin's theory of schizophrenia held the premise that it was a result of the disintegration of attention, or the way that attention became skewed in the mind of the schizophrenic.

Principle of "creative synthesis" (Schöpferische Synthese)

This principle of creative synthesis would eventually become known as the principle of creative resultants. Wundt first referred to it in 1862, and it formed the core of his ideas even to his death. This concept states that such sensations as color, touches, musical tones, and words of speech are subjective reactions of the brain rather than either an interpretation of what has been put into the brain by stimulus or the taking in and storing of something brought into the brain from outside. Such reactions are what he called creative synthesis. One of Wundt's biographers noted:

> Sense organ and neural events may be described endlessly in terms of physics and chemistry, but such descriptions do not include (do not produce for us) the actual psychological qualities known as "sweet," "sour," "heavy," "dark blue," "dazzling crimson," "sharp," "painful," or "meaningful." To get those qualities you must have a living brain, one that is awake, conscious, and attentive, i.e., a brain that is reacting and having experiences.

Wundt continually expanded upon this principle throughout his life.

Explanation In his autobiography, Wundt explained the thought process that led him to the notion of creative synthesis. He recalled that when he "first approached psychological problems," he "shared the general prejudice natural to physiologists that the formation of perceptions is merely the work of the physiological properties" of the sense organs. And he went on to say that:

> Then through the examination of visual phenomena I learned to conceive of perception as an act of *creative synthesis.*

> This gradually became my guide, at the hand of which I arrived at a psychological understanding of the development of the higher functions of imagination and intellect. The older psychology gave me no help in this.

Example Wundt's theory of creative synthesis gradually evolved during his first years in Leipzig. He became more focused on emotions and motivation, as well as on volition, since these issues challenged his ideas of creative synthesis. He wrote in 1880 that "The course of both general and individual development shows that desires or urges (the German word, *Triebe*) are the fundamental psychological phenomena from which all mental processes derive." As Wundt was continually amending the principle to broaden its scope, eventually Wundt and his researchers reached their conclusion, which diverted from the conventional wisdom; namely, that consciousness was not simply the sum of its parts. Consciousness itself was seen a process that had two different stages: 1) a large-capacity short-term memory (at one time referred to as "the Blickfeld") and, 2) a narrow-capacity focus of selective attention, sometimes known as apperception, and manifested through effort. The latter travels through short-term memory.

Principles of psycholinguistics

Wundt's psychology found its greatest success and acceptance within the field of language. As a consequence, Wundt and his colleagues set forth a linguistic theory that was very detailed and comprehensive and resulted from their psychological principles. By the beginning of the twentieth century, many linguistics scholars and psychologists, especially in America, had adhered to Wundt's extensive writings on the subject. He first presented his ideas on the psychology of language in his initial lecture upon arriving in Leipzig in 1875. In 1883, in his *Logik,* he wrote extensively on language for the first time in publication. The first two books of his *Volkerpsychologie (Folk Psychology),* published in 1900, contained his treatise on linguistics and language performance. The section, entitled, "Die Sprache (Language)," was revised in 1904 and further revised and expanded in 1911–12.

Explanation One biographer noted that the key to understanding Wundt's linguistic theories is the concept that "syntax, the sound systems, and all structures in language are seen as taking their particular form by virtue of the operating characteristics of underlying universal mental processes." According to Wundt, the mechanisms of attention, short-term memory, cognitive time limits, and self-control formed the foundation of language. Language's basic unit was the sentence, which served to identify a specific mental state. It represented the way in which the central focal attention process divides and subdivides mental impressions, with an understanding of the relationship between those divisions. No element of language—words or any other building block—

could have any meaning except as it was connected to that relationship with the mental sentence that provided the reason for it.

Example Based on his theory, Wundt and others studied language, particularly that of children. Before a child would begin to speak, the impact of emotional gestures and sounds would have begun to form language and the basis for it. As a child was able to increase the focus of attention on emotional urges, the mental activity providing for the creation of sentences would have begun to produce the elements necessary for language.

Wundt contributed to another popular twentieth-century focus of education, tree diagrams, which became a standard form of diagramming sentences. These diagrams formed a shape like a pyramid, starting at the top, in order to show the distinction between the subject and predicate of the sentence. Subject and predicate could be further divided and subdivided into other parts of speech. In his *Sprachpsychologie,* Wundt explained this by noting that the sentence was

> not an image running with precision through consciousness where each single word or single sound appears only momentarily while the preceding and following elements are lost from consciousness. Rather, it stands as a whole at the cognitive level while it is being spoken.

His idea was that a sentence was not a "chain of

words or word concepts."

The emotion system

Wundt offered his studied beliefs regarding the emotions in contrast to other theorists of the day, all of whom worked in the traditions of either romanticism or rationalism. Wundt sided more with the principles of romanticism, meaning that human beings fall into the category of emotional beings rather than intellectual.

Explanation Contemporaries such as William James, who were transforming such romantic tradition into a modern-day behaviorism, took exception to Wundt's approach. But Wundt noted,

> First, the definite outer symptoms of emotions do not appear until such time as the psychical nature of the emotion is already clearly established. The emotions, accordingly, precedes the innervation [a stimulation that results in movement] effects which are looked upon by these investigators as causes of emotion. Second, it is absolutely impossible to classify the rich variety of psychical emotional states in the comparatively simple scheme of innervation changes. The psychical processes are much more varied than are their accompanying forms of expression. Third, and finally, the physical concomitants stand in no constant

relation to the psychical quality of the emotions. This holds especially for the effects on pulse and respiration, but is true also for the pantomimetic expressive movements. It may sometimes happen that emotions with very different, even opposite kinds of affective contents may belong to the same class so far as the accompanying physical phenomena are concerned.

When Wundt referred to "feelings," "moods," and "emotions," he was not specifying categories, only intensity levels. He would later present his ideas about sensory qualities, explaining affective and aesthetic qualities of experience.

Example Wundt held to the idea that all mental states were transported through constant fluctuations of emotions, mood, or feeling. Sometimes these would become intense enough to precipitate action. Inherent in every mood, according to Wundt, was its opposite. Other psychologists moved out of the context of Wundt's ideas to provided their own generation of his tridimensional feelings. The three dimensions were ideas to which others basically adhered. The aspects of "pleasure versus displeasure," "high versus low arousal," and "concentrated versus relaxed attention" were explained further by the notions of the opposites of control, potency, and domination as opposed to submission. An example he used when discussing sensory qualities were a person's reactions to music and rhythms.

The volition system

Through the intensive reaction-time research program Wundt established at Leipzig, he and his fellow researchers were able to study what he called "decision and choice." Simply stated, they attempted to analyze volition, or self-control. Kurt Danziger published the first English account of the research in 1989, previously published only by the philosopher Theodore Mischel, who published in a philosophy journal and whose work was not known to psychologists.

Explanation Wundt did not believe that emotions were sensations, or caused by external stimulus activity. He was convinced that they were internal products of the central nervous system with no other influences. Emotional forces were internal forces, ever-changing, and just features of consciousness. Wundt used the terms "volition" and "motivation" interchangeably with emotions. He thought that what might have been the controlled or voluntary efforts in primal beings could have become automatic mechanisms as humans evolved. Wundt did believe that in such highly evolved creatures as modern humans, "pure impulses or drives" could be contained by attentional control, and consequently become conscious volitions. A biographer noted:

> The automatization of actions, mental or otherwise is, however, a double-edged sword. Rapid articulate speech, for example, is a largely automatized process, but when we focus too intently

on some motive or extraneous thought while speaking, we are in danger of losing control of the articulation process.

Human beings must continually refocus in order to keep control of the automatic control "wiring" that is inherent. If it is not "tuned up" lapses occur, just as short-term memory can fade without the appropriate mental exercises.

In discussing these automatic behaviors further, Wundt wrote that,

It is not improbable that all the reflex movements of both animals and men originate in this way. As evidence of this we have, besides the above described reduction of volitional acts through practice to pure mechanical processes, also the *purposeful character of reflexes,* which points to the presence at some time of purposive ideas as motives.

Another biographer observed, "Like most of his other theories, Wundt's views on volition were subject to periodic revision. However, once he had developed the independent position of his mature years, these revisions did not affect his fundamental views."

Example The automatic behaviors can be witnessed in considering the skills a person possesses when heading into the study of advanced math. Had the student not learned the basic rules of algebra so that its operations were automatic, the more complicated steps of higher mathematics would be virtually impossible. The same is true in writing and forming grammatical sentences. The mechanical aspect of language becomes so automatic that the writer can simply focus on content rather than the process—just as in conversations, when a person does not have to stop and focus on each step of the process, but rather only on what is being said. Still another example of this concept is the pianist who has developed the skill of playing well enough to talk or sing simultaneously, focusing on that behavior rather than the mechanics of playing. People experience such behavior daily even as they lock their houses when they leave, for instance, or do not stop to think how to open their garage doors, instead, simply pressing the opener automatically as they approach their house.

Apperception concept

Basically defined, apperception referred to the process of focusing on a particular content in consciousness. This term more specifically described the psychological processes that explained what was involved in patterns of deliberate, voluntary actions.

Explanation Within Wundt's concept of the process of mental functions was included, as in his other theories, the polar opposite to the main focus. In other words, he described the point of focus as well as the rest of the field of consciousness. The polarization is the result of the process of apperception, which was a manifestation of volition. Apperception was the principle that motivated and provided experience to both direction and structure. It also indicated a "central" process that could operate in two directions, on sensory content that could result in more complex forms of perception, and on the shaping of ideas. While that idea was not so revolutionary, Wundt's additional notion of the opposite, that apperception also operated on the motor apparatus, was more innovative. This idea meant that not only was the mind constructed with regard to focus and the field that surrounded it, but the actual movement of the body and the skeleton also functioned in the same way, by selectively controlling movements.

By the third edition of his *Principles of Physiological Psychology,* Wundt revised his concept of apperception even more. He offered the distinction between what he termed "impulsive" apperception, involving the motor direction of apperception; and "reproductive" apperception, indicating cognitive direction. Impulsive apperception, the controlling process, directly affects the motor apparatus. One of Wundt's biographers explained that during the process of development, "movement images are eventually formed by the differentiation and recombination of movement sensations." In reproductive apperception, those movements can be recalled. It involves only the memory of the movement, and not the movement process itself.

Examples The sucking of an infant on the mother's

breast would be just one such impulsive movement. Such "primitive" activities indicated that the central stimulus would immediately and directly result in particular patterns of motor behavior. The biographer noted, "But such motor activity leads necessarily to the formation of motor images (no matter how rudimentary) which can be recalled by reproductive apperception." With the way these activities can blend together, or fuse, and with the activities of analysis and consequent recombination, as Wundt saw it, new movements can be created.

Summary

In an 1894 autobiographical statement reflecting on his life's work, Wundt wrote that

If I were asked what I thought the value for psychology of the experimental method was in the past and still is, I would answer that for me it created and continues to confirm a wholly new view of the nature and interrelations of mental processes. When I first approached psychological problems, I shared the general prejudice natural to physiologists that the formation of perceptions is merely the work of the physiological properties of our sense organs. Then through the examination of visual phenomena I learned to conceive of perception as an act of *creative synthesis.* This gradually became my guide, at the hand of which I arrived at a psychological understanding of the development of the higher functions of imagination and intellect. The older psychology gave me no help in this. When I then proceeded to investigate the temporal relations in the flow of mental events, I gained a new insight into the development of volition ... an insight likewise into the similarity of mental functions which are artificially distinguished by abstractions and name— such as "ideas," "feelings," or "will." In a word, I glimpsed the indivisibility of mental life, and saw its similarity on all its levels. The chronometric investigation of associative processes showed me the relation of perceptual processes to memory images. It also taught me to recognize that the concept of "reproduced" ideas is one of the many fictions that has become set in our language to create a picture of something that does not exist in reality. I learned to understand that "mental representation" is a process which is no less changing and transient than a feeling or an act of will. As a consequence of all this I saw the old theory of association is no longer tenable. It must be replaced by the notion of relational processes involving rudimentary feelings, a view that results in giving up the stable linkages and close connections of successive as well as simultaneous associations.

HISTORICAL CONTEXT

Wundt's life spanned 88 years. The world into which he was born in 1832 was certainly very different from the world in which he died—a post-World War I Germany. Europe was undergoing enormous political and physical changes. The landscape of what had been a continent of small kingdoms and tiny countries had evolved into a Europe of fewer countries and more deadly wars. Greece had become an independent state. Prince Otto of Wittlesbach became King of Bavaria before that nation joined a unified Germany. The medieval cannon-and-sword warfare had evolved into the airplanes, bombs, and the battles of a new century. Medical and scientific advances were slowly making the world a place with increasing life expectancy, wider opportunities for travel, and more accessible education to a class of people who could not have hoped for such intellectual adventures just decades earlier. The industrial revolution had swept through Europe first, and then the United States, bringing about technological capabilities that few had ever dreamed possible. The year Wundt was born, Michael Faraday's laws of electrolysis were made public. In 1839, when Wundt was only seven years old, Louis-Jacques-Mand Daguerre developed the first photographic images. By the time of Wundt's death, the average person could operate handheld cameras and view motion pictures. This period of significant social change caused a shift in in human consciousness as well—people began to view themselves as living within an ever-changing context.

Although Wundt spent a great deal of time alone throughout his childhood, he could not ignore the significance of what was going on in the world around him. Those events affected him and helped to shape the path he would follow into his profession. Just as his own personal life and development gave cause to his life of research and experiment, so did the changing world around him, especially in academia, medicine, and politics. While serving on the faculty at the university, Wundt also served as an elected representative from his district in Heidelberg, for the Baden diet (governing body), beginning on April 26, 1866. He would resign about 18 months later because he did not believe the life of his research would be compatible with the necessary demands of political life. He would become a champion for German unification. Wundt gave a speech to the Heidelberg branch of the Workers' Educational League in 1864, the text of which was found among his papers after his death. One of his biographers documented

> Wundt stated that the goal of the entire working-class movement was the freedom and independence of the working class and its salvation from mechanization, but that this goal was indissolubly linked to German unity and freedom. German workers must therefore rise above their class interests, to fight

with a sense of duty for the honor of the nation. Strength in warfare and soundness of character are independent of privilege, Wundt said, and they have more value than gold or possessions.

In his professional life, Wundt was first and foremost an innovator who followed no other trends. He was influenced by such great thinkers as Dutch philosopher Benedict de Spinoza—especially his idea of psychophysical parallelism that stated every physical event has a mental counterpart and vice versa—and his teachers and mentors such as Johannes Müller, Du Bois-Reymond, and Hermann von Helmholtz.

As Wundt was beginning his career at Heidelberg as an assistant to Helmholtz, an other great thinker, Gustav Theodor Fechner (1801–87) was finishing his work, *Elemente.* The Prussian-born scientist, who had studied medicine followed by mathematics and physics, was credited with presenting the formal beginning of experimental psychology. In *Serendip,* in a discussion entitled, "Mind, Brain, and the Experimental Psychology of Consciousness," the author stated that

> While the philosophical message of the *Elemente* was largely ignored, its methodological and empirical contributions were not. Fechner may have set out to counter materialist metaphysics; but he was a well-trained, systematic experimentalist and a

competent mathematician and the impact of his work on scientists such as Helmholtz, Ernst Mach, A.W. Volkmann, Delboeuf, and others was scientific rather than metaphysical. By combining methodological innovation in measurement with careful experimentation, Fechner moved beyond Herbart to answer Kant's second object regarding the possibility of scientific psychology. Mental events could, Fechner showed, not only be measured, but measured in terms of their relationship to physical events. In achieving this milestone, Fechner demonstrated the potential for quantitative, experimental exploration of the phenomenology of sensory experience and established psychophysics as one of the core methods of the newly emerging scientific psychology.

Wundt was ready to explore this changing climate. He agreed with Fechner, noted a biographer, that "the availability of measurable stimuli (and reactions) could make psychological events open to something like experimental methodology in a way earlier philosophers such as Kant thought impossible."

While he was assistant to Helmholtz, Wundt actually conducted most of his experiments at home, on his own time. Though psychology and psychiatry were both required medical school courses, Wundt first used the word psychology, in a course title in 1862. That would mark the true beginning for him of what would become a prolific writing career as well as that of experimental psychology. When he set up his first makeshift lab in 1875 for his demonstrations of sensation and perception, Wundt was sharing a stage only with William James at Harvard, who had embarked upon a similar path. On March 24, 1879, Wundt formally requested funds from the Royal Saxon Ministry of Education in order to set up and support a lab with psychophysical apparatus. Wundt was not granted the allocation. But two of his students, American G. Stanley Hall and fellow German Max Friedrich, nonetheless began their scientific investigations in a small classroom that had once been given to Wundt for storage. Until that time, psychology had no prominent place in the academic or scientific world. It had been relegated to either the philosophy or the natural sciences departments.

Wundt was influenced by German philosophical thought of the era. At the time, German philosophy held to the idea that sensations were psychological events, and thus internal to the mind. But sensation related to something that was external to the mind. With that disposition, Wundt's introspection was what modern-day philosophers or psychologists might call observation. A biographer wrote that Wundt's psychology was a "major occupant of that relatively brief period when the shape of modern psychology was still wide open." Contemporary to Wundt, and influencing his approach, were the British associationists and the German Herbartians (followers of philosopher Johann Friedrich Herbart). He concluded, along with them, that all psychology began in the conscious experience of individual human subjects. He gave the British the credit for being the first to develop a psychological system based on that premise. Yet, the same biographer noted that although Herbart had made some changes to the British system, "the very achievements of both these earlier forms of psychology had led to a new set of problems." He went to say "Their contributions had been indispensable in demolishing the legacy of faculty psychology, but the theoretical constructions with which they replaced the latter were base on fundamental errors and illusions."

In his psychology journal, *Philosophische Studien,* which he founded in 1881, Wundt again proved to be a pioneer. The journal was the first of its kind. If Wundt built on the foundation of what a few others had established, he also became the starting point for generations of other, world-famous psychologists, and many more people for whom experimental psychology would set the trends for a new century.

CRITICAL RESPONSE

The immediate critical response to Wundt's work, *Grundzuge der physiologischen Psychologie,* was strongly favorable. The reviews of the book appeared everywhere, and the discussions it prompted were dynamic. Students throughout the world who began to read it were immediately captivated—from Germany, from the United States, from England—and they all rushed to Wundt's classroom and the early versions of his laboratory. Following the initial fascination and praise, as time progressed the inevitable ideological battles arose. Cultural differences altered the unified voice of interest. Perhaps the most profound tribute would eventually be that so many branches of his theories spawned new fields of study—of both digression and support. In this way, Wundt played the vital role of beginning discussions that continued into the twenty-first century, debates that hinged on the understanding of valid scientific study.

Wundt was presenting a new science of psychology, ready to take its place among physics, chemistry, and biology. That reality often was lost, however, amidst the overwhelming number of his publications. A biographer noted,

> Certainly not the least reason for neglect of the whole Wundtian *corpus* is the challenge of sheer quantity. Wundt's academic career was huge—sixty years

of productivity, 17,000 students, the all-time winner in the academic ritual of "publish-or-perish." Who could be surprised that the later recollections (Wundt memorial publications), appearing in several countries shortly after his death, suggest the fable of the blind men feeling different parts of an elephant? One need mention only those dozens of American college boys who sailed off for a year or two at Leipzig in the late nineteenth century. They were armed merely with a semester of two of college German and an American small-college degree—hardly a match for the formidable academic preparation of German *Gymnasium* students.

Especially with some of these young Americans, as well as those other non-German speaking students, the debate over Wundt's work and what it was or was not grew particularly heated in the early years of World War I (1914–18).

Some of the criticism leveled at Wundt accused him as a representative of his nation's "evil" culture. Even American journalist H. L. Mencken (1880–1956) weighed in on the matter. He observed in the mid-1920s about the challenges of Americans translating German, and said that

The average American professor is far too dull a fellow to undertake so difficult an enterprise. Even when he sports a

German Ph.D. one usually finds out on examination that all he knows about modern German literature is that a *Mass* of Hofbrau in Munich used to cost 27 *Pfennig* downstairs and 32 *Pfenning* upstairs. The German universities were formerly very tolerant of foreigners. Many an American, in preparation for professoring at Harvard, spent a couple of years roaming from one to the other of them without picking up enough German to read the *Berliner Tageblatt.* Such frauds swarm in all our lesser universities, and many of them, during the war, became eminent authorities upon the crimes of [philosopher Friedrich] Nietzsche and the errors of [historian Heinrich von] Treitschke.

Any interpretation or criticism of Wundt must be mindful of this American attitude.

Also at the time of Wundt's first major publication of the *Physiological Psychology,* a review in the *Literarisches Centralblatt* in 1874 said that the book, "corresponds exactly to the need created by recent developments in physiology and psychology and the [consequent] lively demand for a *specialized* scientific treatment of the actual relations between body and consciousness." British psychologist James Sully in 1876, unlike William James, would write that he did accept the fact that Wundt had "defined the boundaries of a new department of research in Germany." He also complimented Wundt for "putting into systematic form the results of a number of more or less isolated inquiries." His colleague Friedrich Lange found Wundt's work so impressive that he recommended Wundt for the chair of inductive philosophy at Zurich University, even when Wundt's academic career had otherwise been undistinguished and lacked the fame that others in his field were enjoying.

One observer agreed with the perspective that provided an important clue in how to approach Wundt's critics, both contemporary and modern. He noted in 2000 that the world was beginning to notice Wundt again, and his work was beginning a new surge in popularity. Boeree reflected:

> Over 100 years after his work, we have finally caught up with him . . . Actually, he was massively misrepresented by poorly educated American students in Germany, and especially a rather ego-driven Englishman named Titchener. Wundt recognized that Titchener was misrepresenting him, and tried to make people aware of the problem. But Boring —the premier American historian of psychology for many decades—only knew Wundt through Titchener.

Much of the problem lay in the mistranslation, or the lack of translation of his works, especially for the English-speaking audience. The title itself of his *Principles of Physiological Psychology,* gave first witness to the issue. "Physiological" was a term that originally meant "experimental" but that used the methods of the physiology laboratory. Especially upon the advent of the behaviorists in the twentieth century, the confusion over the essence of Wundt's psychological theories would only increase before the real message of his work would be made clear.

This problem continued with various biographical profiles that inevitably list his greatest achievement as the establishment of experimental methods rather than his theories themselves. For instance, Zusne wrote in 1984 that Wundt's "systematic views are of lesser importance and constitute largely a descriptive system." Indeed, his work in establishing his lab alone was a significant achievement that would serve as a tribute to Wundt throughout the rest of history. Zusne was mistaken when he noted in his biographical profile of Wundt that "Wundt's elementism and the method of introspection did not survive the death of his truest disciple, E. B. Titchener." But even Zusne agreed that the path leading away from Wundt's laboratories into those of pioneering psychologists throughout the world found a basis in his theories. In establishing branches of applied psychology, others would use his theories to grow into branches from the seed Wundt planted, even though he did not believe in applied psychology himself.

Wundt's theory of emotions and creative synthesis would provide a cornerstone for the Gestalt school of psychology. His student Emil Kraepelin would use the basic tenets of Wundt's actuality principle and its descriptions of processes of central selective attention to form his own theory of schizophrenia in 1917.

Another biographer offered a different analysis of Wundt and the interpretations of his work. He wrote that:

> But the difficulties of Wundt scholarship are not entirely a matter of translation. Some of them are intrinsic to the original texts. Wundt was virtually encyclopedic in his writings with the result that he would often discuss topics in different contexts and therefore arrive at somewhat different formulations. That can make it difficult to extract the definitive Wundt position on specific issues.

Wundt's long life and career complicated matters as well. Throughout the course of his work, some of his opinions changed due to the evolution of his own theories and experimentation methods. He was known to be sometimes reluctant to admit he had changed his mind, and the result was ongoing confusion about what he believed.

James, Hall, and the American school

As a group, the hundreds of young Americans who studied with Wundt were only part of the consideration of the impact he made in America. Certain Americans, professors and scholars such as

William James and G. Stanley Hall, merited a closer study. These people were the movers of thought in the United States, and far more significant in the debate about Wundt. In his own review of Wundt's first work, James was very favorable. He welcomed it as a book "indispensable for study and reference," even if it did have many shortcomings, in his opinion. "But, they [the shortcomings] only prove how confused and rudimentary the science of psychophysics still is," he added. Only later would James come to criticize Wundt for those shortcomings, as well as the different courses their philosophies took them (see accompanying sidebar).

Because James and Wundt were contemporaries who had studied with some of the same giants in the early years of physiological and psychological research, contrasting their views is essential to studying the arguments of Wundt. G. Stanley Hall's perspectives on Wundt are also useful, since not only had Hall studied with Wundt, but he also had taken what he knew back to America to begin a similar research path.

Often the focus of the debate between Wundt and James centers on the structuralist approach of Wundt compared to the functionalism of James. A writer noted that the two schools of thought were actually more similar to each other than to the rest of mainstream psychology. Both, he pointed out, were engaged in the principle of free will and opposed to the materialistic philosophy. Even their ideas of what made psychology worth studying, as well as the nature of its essence, did not differ much.

In comparing their ideas, it is helpful to consider the following points made by that writer. For Wundt:

> "Mind," "intellect," "reason," "understanding," *etc.* are concepts that existed before the advent of any scientific psychology. The fact that the naive consciousness always and everywhere points to internal experience as a special source of knowledge may, therefore, be accepted for the moment as sufficient testimony to the right of psychology as a science. "Mind" will accordingly be the subject to which we attribute all the separate facts of internal observation as predicates. The subject itself is determined wholly and exclusively by its predicates.

What James offered to make a similar point was that, "There is only one primal stuff or material in the world, a stuff of which everything is composed, and we call that stuff, 'pure experience.'"

Neither Wundt nor James were proponents of the Hegelian system of rationale, however, or other such philosophical ideas. They were similar, too, in the way they viewed materialism and reductionism. Wundt wrote:

> If we could see every wheel in the physical mechanism whose working the

mental processes are accompanying, we should still find no more than a chain of movements showing no trace whatsoever of their significance for mind. All that is valuable in our mental life still falls to the psychical side.

The doctrine of materialism was equally distasteful to James, a follower of pragmatism, and a student of Charles Sanders Peirce, who had founded that philosophy. But James did not give credence to Wundt's introspection of consciousness. His own thoughts led him to focus on behavior in outer environments, though James would scarcely have believed that behaviorist psychology evolved from his own philosophy.

G. Stanley Hall commented in one paragraph about Wundt, in 1920, the year of Wundt's death, that

> Wundt has had for decades the prestige of a most advantageous academic chair. He founded the first laboratory for experimental psychology, which attracted many of the most gifted and mature students from all lands. By his development of the doctrine of apperception he took psychology forever beyond the old associationism which had ceased to be fruitful. He also established the independence of psychology from physiology, and by his encyclopaedic and always thronged lectures, to say nothing

of his more or less esoteric seminary, he materially advanced every branch of natural sciences and extended its influence over the whole wide domain of folklore, mores, language, and primitive religion. His best texts will long constitute a thesaurus which every psychologist must know.

In the next paragraph, however, he went on to offer harsh criticism, saying that Wundt had suffered from a narrow approach in his attempt to understand the human mind. In his discussion of what was on the horizon with Freud as compared to Wundt, Hall added that, "We cannot forebear to express the hope that Freud will not repeat Wundt's error in making too abrupt a break with his more advanced pupils like Adler or the Zurich group." Hall believed that, had Wundt spent more time studying biology and less time studying physics and physiology, he might have looked in greater depth at the theory of evolution or the role that genetics played in "psychic powers and activities." Hall's criticisms of Wundt came much later in his life, however; he had been very complimentary during most of his career.

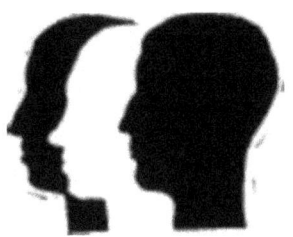

BIOGRAPHY:
William James

As a contemporary of Wilhelm Wundt who studied physiology with many of the same people, including Helmholtz at the University of Heidelberg, William James (1842–1910) was considered the founder of American psychology. Even into the twenty-first century, he has retained his reputation as America's foremost psychologist. James was also known as a member of the pragmatist movement, which was founded by philosopher Charles Peirce. James held little respect for Wundt, however, and he challenged the claim that Wundt's experimental laboratory was the first of its kind. James established his lab at Harvard in 1875, although his research did not generate the intense interest that Wundt's did. Historical records have placed the opening of Wundt's famous Leipzig lab in 1879; he joined the Leipzig faculty in 1875, however, and began conducting his first experiments there.

William James was born a child of privilege on January 11, 1842, in New York City, the eldest son of Henry James, Sr. and Mary R. Walsh James. His grandfather, also named William James, had been a successful land speculator; he amassed a significant fortune, estimated at approximately 3 million dollars when he died in 1832. Henry, Sr. was well known for his salon for intellectuals and his somewhat renegade theology as a Swedenborgian, practitioners of Protestant Christianity who were very much caught up in religious mysticism. His brother Henry would eventually become famous in his own right as a novelist who chronicled the lives of wealthy Americans at home and abroad. James and his siblings enjoyed traveling to Europe, spoke both German and French, and were well-versed in artistic pursuits.

James enrolled at Harvard at the age of 19 as a chemistry student. He changed his major to medicine within a very short time, even though his real interest was science. When he was 21, in 1865, James had the opportunity to study along the Amazon River, traveling with the famous biologist Louis Agassiz, who was collecting samples of new species. In 1867 he traveled to Germany to study physiology. During his studies in Germany, he showed his first signs of serious depression, even harboring thoughts of suicide, as well as suffering from other health problems. He returned to the United States in 1869 to complete his medical degree. Reading a French philosopher named Renouvier helped James become a believer in the power of free will. As he adopted this belief to address his own problems, he thought his life and health might be improving.

James received his M.D. from Harvard in 1869; his Ph.D. and Litt.D., from Padua (Italy) in 1893; and an LL.D. from Princeton in 1896. His professional career was based at Harvard, where he began working in 1872 as an instructor in physiology. He taught physiology, psychology, and philosophy at Harvard—eventually becoming a professor —until 1907. He was a professor emeritus at Harvard from 1907 until his death in 1910. His major work was, *Principles of Psychology,* a book that James wrote over a 12-year period. A key theory he espoused therein would eventually become known as functionalism—his opposition to the structuralism of such psychologists as Wundt. Among his many other writings are *The Will to Believe,* published in 1897; *Varieties of Religious Experience,* 1902; *Pragmatisim,* 1907, which popularized the theory as a practical way to lead a useful life; and *The Meaning of Truth,* 1909. That same year he published, *Pluralistic Universe,* which contained some additional ideas of pragmatism. While recognized more for being a teacher and celebrity, rather than for the substance of his beliefs, James solidified his prominent reputation in American psychology.

James married Alice Gibbens in 1878, and the couple had five children. He died on August 26, 1910, at the family home in Chocorua, New Hampshire, after several years of suffering from heart problems.

The real breakdown between Wundt and his structuralism, and the Americans and their functionalism, was mostly due to the way Wundt's and others' theories were melded into the American culture. A 1969 book described the controversy by noting that:

Functionalism *did* make its appearance as a psychology of protest. Its leaders *did* oppose the school that was then the establishment in American psychology: the classical experimentalists, essentially Wundtian in outlook, who saw as their basic and immediate scientific task the introspective analysis of conscious experiences under experimentally controlled conditions. These were its psychologists, who, during the ensuing controversy, came to be called structuralists. And the functionalists *did* place more emphasis on the study of behavior than the classical experimentation has accorded it. Without denying introspection a legitimate and useful role, the functionalists in their own researches drew heavily on behavioral data. Influenced as they were by Darwinian theory, they undertook investigations that required that most, and in some cases all of the empirical data be obtained from the study of behavior—researched in developmental psychology, in educational and other forms of applied psychology, and in animal psychology, to mention a few examples.

Another observer's view of the debate and antagonism between the Americans and Wundt was that it was "no confrontation at all in one aspect and a misfired polemic [argument] in another." Again, this writer criticized Titchener, among others, as a factor in the debate when he went on to say that:

It [the functionalist/structuralist debate] was begun by a humanist, who found the Newtonian interpretations of science brought to this country by Wundt's students lacking in something vital to [man's] conceptualization. Titchener lost the totality (the one) in the constitutive total of basal elements (the many), and yet this self-organizing principle of mental life is most characteristic of the human experience. Rather than a full airing of the introspective-versus-extraspective *theoretical* slant implied, what developed was a temporary quibble over the rules of *methodological* procedure.

Other Americans who had once praised Wundt would eventually criticize him. These included James Mark Baldwin, who constantly referred to Wundt in his 1889 *Handbook of Psychology,* but barely mentioned him in his 1913 *History of Psychology,* except to criticize his "tendency to abstract classification and schematicism," in *Volkerpsychologie.*

Wundt's American loyalists One former student of Wundt, an American named Edward Wheeler Scripture, would eventually Americanize some of Wundt's methods enough to use them for application with time-and-motion studies in industrial psychology and clinical applications for work with communication disorders. Scripture worked at the Yale Psychology Laboratory under the supervision of George T. Ladd. The two men were in continual conflict due to their philosophical conflicts. Scripture was to a great extent loyal to Wundt's teachings; Ladd apparently was not.

Charles Herbert Judd, one of the German psychology professor's American students, was named by one author as "by far the most loyal American student of Wundt." Judd took over control of the Yale lab when Scripture and Ladd were both fired for their conflict. But, again, with the Americanization process occurring in the form that application was taking in the United States, especially in the educational psychology—a field that with Hall's help was beginning to boom by the early years of the twentieth century—even a loyalist like Judd would eventually fall in line with the application theorists.

In 1912, Hall wrote about Wundt, again showing the conflicts that his former students had felt about the changes that experimental psychology had effected. Hall pondered:

> Perhaps what is now needed is another Wundt with another life . . . perhaps it is a bold synthetic genius who will show us the way out . . . It would seem as if laboratory psychology in this country was now sufficiently developed so that it should be less dependent upon the new departures made in Germany. The present impasse is the most challenging opportunity ever presented to psychologists. In this crisis our need is a new method, point of view, assortment of topics and problems. These, I believe, geneticism is very soon to supply. Meanwhile, we may have at least for a time to follow Wirth's call to go back to Wundt.

Wundt influenced many European contemporaries such as Belgian phenomenologist Albert Michotte (1881–1965). In much the same roles Wundt and James had played in their respective countries, Michotte was considered the founder of Belgian experimental psychology. He had studied with Wundt in Leipzig during the 1905–06 academic terms, inspired to pursue the issue of voluntary choice. Eventually he would become known especially for his research into the "perception of causality," and the direction he would provide to the later Gestalt psychologists. Michotte's work would also be an important stepping stone to the birth of the field of social psychology. Another Belgian, George Dwelshauvers (1866–1937) was a strong advocate of experimental psychology. He worked at Wundt's Institute in Leipzig after he received his doctorate in Brussels. He returned there in 1889, intending to open a psychological institute. He wrote to Wundt, explaining that in doing so he would "let the true way of experimental psychology rescue his 'extremely unphilosophical country' from the 'ridiculous masquerades' of the 'spiritualists, positivists, and materialists'."

Wilhelm Wirth (1876–1952) took a position as an assistant to Wundt at Leipzig in 1900. He would eventually become known for his work in psychophysics. But after his arrival, he became one of Wundt's foremost defenders through his experimental work. The results he obtained supported Wundt when his critics were mounting the case against his methods and theories. That was also the time when his reaction-time studies had begun a resurgence. Following Wundt's retirement in 1917, however, Wirth left to pursue his own work in psychophysics. He would no longer carry much influence at Leipzig, especially in psychology, in the way his director once had.

Interest in Wundt experienced a serious revival in the 1970s, after his large contribution in psycholinguistics was rediscovered. A 1979 profile of Wundt for the American Psychological Association's *Contemporary Psychology,* series was entitled the "The founding father we never knew." The debate the review inspired led to the revised view of Wundt taken by twenty-first century psychology.

Scholars have continued to examine Wundt's work a century after his death. The intricacies of understanding he brought to the study of human consciousness might not ever be totally decipherable. But it is clear that his significance continued, as advancements in technology brought an entirely new direction in the study of the human brain and how it works.

Important beginning

The significance of Wundt's work and his place as a pioneer cannot be overstated. One observer wrote that, "The reaction-time studies conducted during the first few years of Wundt's laboratory constituted the first historical example of a coherent research program, explicitly directed toward psychological issues and involving a number of interlocking studies."

Another author stated:

One very important endeavor in Wundt's scientific work was to study the facts pertaining to the nature of the human organism, to isolate these facts by observation, and to measure them in terms of intensity and duration, that is to say, to study the psychic compounds formed by and revealed to us by our "introspective experience."

Wundt was an experimental psychologist. That meant that he was not sitting in a room listening to a client's problems, for instance, or helping direct a changed path in a client's life following some childhood trauma. It was Wundt's business to try to take apart the human psyche in the same way a mechanic might dismantle an automobile's engine and operating system. An explanation of Wundt's research and experiments serves as a necessary component to the observation of the theories that might have evolved from those experiments.

Research

Psychology historian Edwin G. Boring offered readers a description of what went on in Wundt's laboratory. Boring was able to classify 109 experimental articles from Wundt's journal, *Philosophische Studien,* into four categories.

The four categories, along with the percentage of the body of work they represented, were:

- Sensation and perception, over 50%.
- Reaction times (mostly before 1890), less than 20%.
- Attention and feeling (mostly in the 1890s), 10%.
- Association, less than 10%.

In the first category, the study of vision predominated the studies of sensation and perception, followed by auditory perception. Tactile sensation, although a crucial study area in the history of psychophysics, was the topic of only a few of the research studies. No articles were published on the sense of smell, and only a few on the sense of taste. Three researchers studied what Boring referred to as the "sixth sense" or the "time sense," in their experiments on the perception, or estimation of time intervals. Another historian explained that:

> As a specialist in sensory perception, Boring strongly identified with the Wundtian experimental tradition. Although he suggested that reaction–time experiments were part of the core of the work of the early Institute, he concluded that this line of research ultimately failed when it proved impossible to measure separately the times required by discrete mental functions. The failure was by no means total, as Metge (1983) has argued [Anneros Metge, "The experimental psychological research conducted at Wundt's Institute and its significance in the history of psychology," in the book, *Advances in historiography of psychology*.] and Boring neglected to emphasize how important this "failed" program" was to the development of laboratory psychology.

In this case, the importance of Wundt's work was born of unexpected consequences, and it was not even his original intention. As the historian continued:

> When Wundt came to Leipzig, studies of sensation and perception were primarily identified with physiology, and Wundt would change that identification only

partially. Research on sensation and perception in the Leipzig Institute, in the large picture, was preliminary or ancillary to investigations of complex central-nervous processes. Reaction-time experiments sought to measure those processes directly. Leipzig researchers worked in hot pursuit of the parameters and laws of mental chronometry, and Wundt's theory of mental processes implied that reaction-time experiments could serve as the model for investigating many mental phenomena, including attention, will, association, feeling, and emotion.

But the so-called failure, however, led to an entirely new way of psychological experimentation, an outgrowth from the problems of these early experiments.

Wundt was not the first researcher to study reaction times. Early nineteenth-century astronomers, for instance, had continually encountered the phenomenon of the human factor in their quest to gain increasingly accurate simultaneous measurements of position and time for certain celestial events. This human factor would often cause variations of as much as a half-second. Wundt was curious about that difference—enough so that he wanted to explain why such differences existed and provide some standard measurement of reaction times. Thirteen years before he opened his laboratory at Leipzig in 1879, Wundt was credited for his discovery that the "observed time of a reaction was significantly greater than the time required for a nervous impulse to travel from sense organ to the brain plus that required to travel back to the reacting muscle," one biographer observed. That meant the central nervous processes were consuming a lot of the reaction time. Wundt still had to prove it with experimentation, however.

Wundt's instruments and reaction-time experiments A Swiss precision mechanic named Mathias Hipp (1813–1901) developed a measuring instrument for Swiss astronomer Adolph Hirsch (1813–93) who wanted to measure, as one writer reported it, "the speed of thought." The chronoscope, which was a highly precise time clock, could register time intervals to the one–one-thousandth of a second. The instrument remained a laboratory standard for 50 years. In addition to Hirsch, a Dutch psychologist named Franciscus Cornelis Donders (1818–89) had devised the "subtraction method," which utilized the instrument to determine the difference in reaction times from a simple task to a more difficult task. Donders' experiments would help lead Wundt to measuring the focus of his own research—conscious mental actions. The foundation of his work would begin in the reaction-time experiments. American psychologist James McKeen Cattell, who worked in Leipzig on these experiments, helped to clarify the crucial distinction between psychometry and psychophysics in regard to these experiments. In 1888, he wrote that,

We are naturally glad to find it possible to apply methods of measurement directly to consciousness; there is no doubt but that the mental processes take up time, and that this time can be determined. The measurements thus obtained are not psychophysical, as those which we have been recently considering, but purely psychological.

Throughout his research and experimentation, Wundt used a variety of instruments. Ten of those instruments, or similar copies, are housed in the Museum of Psychological Instrumentation at Montclair State University in New Jersey. Edward J. Haupt has copyrighted the captions that accompany their illustration; his basic descriptions are made available on the Web site *PsiCafe,* published by the University of Portland (Oregon) psychology department.

Those particular 10 instruments that are designated as Wundtian, and described in Haupt's words, are:

- Beat (making) apparatus—A drum rotated by weights, and turned in a complete circle in four seconds, with pins on the drum set in row at different distances so that placing the contact on the slider can select different time intervals and thus different intervals between contact closures.

- Eye-motion detector—Demonstrates the

action of the extraocular muscles to move the eyeball.

- Pendulum apparatus—The tool of Wundt's "complication" experiment, with the subject required to visually track the pointer moving across a large dial; it was run with either a visual set or an auditory set, and was a response to an auditory signal; reaction time was longer with the visual set and demonstrated Wundt's "voluntary" action.

- Perimeter—Allowed the presentation of visual stimuli in all parts of the visual field and at a constant distance from the subject's eye; was used to examine visual field for defects and to plot visual acuity and color acuity; an instrument credited to have originated from Helmholtz.

- Rotary apparatus—The "improved" apparatus for the complication experiment, as described in 1902 in one of the last issues of *Philosophische Studien,* with Wundt observers puzzled by his emphasis of the voluntarist or anti-mechanistic conclusions due the fact that no other psychologist or scholar seemed to be interested in that at the time.

- Sound interpreter (pulse generator)— Produced pulse of a certain tone which came through a tube to a rotating disk with 15 precisely-sized holes that each could be filled with a stopper; the speed of the disk was calibrated through a rotation counter; it was a measure of the auditory system.

- Wundt-style tachistoscope—Presented visual stimulus for a very short adjustable exposure time by using a gravity-operated falling shutter; the onset of the shutter's drop was controlled by a solenoid, for vision experimentation.

- Wundt-style chronograph—Claimed time measurements to one–one-thousandth of a second.

- Wundt-style kymograph for experimental plethysmography (measurement to record bodily functions such as the velocity of heart rate, blood flow, and breathing with subsequent changes in the size of limbs and organs)—A soundless instrument up to 100 mm/second in order to determine plethysmographic signal.

- Wundt-style stroboscope—Suitable for exact psychological research, has eight image holders mounted by spring-held clips on eight radial pipes that can be place from 21 to 51 centimeters from the central axis around which the images revolve.

Case studies

As mentioned above, Wundt did use Donders' experiment with the subtraction method, but preferred to do it by means of the Hipp chronoscope rather than the chronograph when he set about his reaction-time studies at Leipzig. Not only did he employ a technical change, Wundt acted on a different concept as well. He believed that a stricter definition between choice and discrimination was vital.

Donders' experiment According to one historian, Donders' experiments relied on "the assumption that each part of the reaction (sensation, perception, discrimination, choice, reaction movement) took a specific amount of time." Speech sounds were the stimulus and the reactions, recorded on a chronograph that was made up of a kymograph, or moving drum, with a tuning fork that marked the drum with the regular vibrations. In this method the differences of the time measurements would be small. The first, or "a" reaction was the simple response to the stimulus; the "b" reaction was that involved with discrimination of the sensory functions, followed by motor selection in telling the researcher what choice had been made; and the "c" reaction held to the discriminatory function but not the motor.

Only five syllables—possible examples would be "ka, ke, ki, ko, ku,"—with particular choices of one of those syllables would comprise a particular reaction. In the case of the simple reaction, both the stimulus and response was "ki;" for the "b" reaction, the stimulus was any of the five syllables with the respondent giving back that same syllable used in the stimulus; in the "c" reaction, the stimulus was any of the five syllables but the respondent was told only to react if hearing the sound of "ki." The last choice indicated that the response involved sensory discrimination but neither motor selection nor choice.

The average reaction time of the results were:

- "a" reaction: 197 milliseconds
- "b" reaction: 285 milliseconds
- "c" reaction: 243 milliseconds

Wundt liked such quantitative results when examining mental processes. Buthe decided that the Donders experiment needed an adjustment. He added a "d" reaction—discrimination without choice. What he was actually proposing here was a true psychological experiment. It was a thought experiment with no external measure as to when such a recognition would occur. Wundt would define a whole new way of experimental psychology with this. His techniques were those of self-observation, inner observation, and inner experience. Wundt held to a model for mental reaction that had five parts.

The five parts were:

- sensation, the movement of the nerve impulse from the sense organ into the brain
- perception, the entry of the signal into the field of consciousness (*Blickfeld des Bewuátseins*)

- apperception, the entry of the signal into the focus of attention (*Blickpunkt des Aufmerksamkeits*)

- act of will, in which the appropriate response signal is released in the brain

- response movement, or more precisely, the movement of the response signal from the brain to where it initiates muscular movement

Steps one and five, Wundt suggested, were purely psychological. The three middle steps were psychosocial because they had both a physiological and a psychic side. All five steps might be contained in a mental reaction. While the middle steps could not be measured, or timed separately, using the subtraction method would provide estimates of the times for apperception, and for an act of will, termed "discrimination time" and "choice time," respectively. For such experimentation, the subjects involved had to be trained in the self-observation that Wundt required so that they could properly report these psychic events.

Wundt's first doctoral students conducted experiments using this method. They followed the discrimination reaction time as it was laid out in his theory. One of the studies that used the visual stimuli had respondents press a key when they perceived a flash of light. Another reaction, the "d" reaction, provided two different images that were suddenly illuminated in front of the subject: either a white circle on black background, or a black circle on white background. As soon as the subject determined what was displayed, he would press a key. The first illumination triggered the Hip chronoscope to run, and pressing the key stopped the dial. The time that elapsed was given as the time of reaction. It is essential to note that Wundt carried out these experiments with his doctoral students Max Friedrich and Ernst Tischer. One acted as the subject, another initiated the reaction, and the third recorded the time. They took turns in different roles. Wundt utilized this model that was representative of the method he preferred to use: a subject, an experimenter, and an observer. The continued this particular experiment until they received an extremely short average time. It turned out to be similar to the result found by Donders: a range of 132 milliseconds (ms) to 226 ms. The "recognition" time added approximately 50 ms, which was Friedrich's average, to 79 ms, which was Wundt's. Using four different colors, the recognition time increased—Tischer's average was 73 ms and Friedrich's was 157 ms.

The results for the first experiment can be summarized as:

- simple reaction: 132–226 ms
- discrimination, two stimuli: 50–79 ms longer
- discrimination, four stimuli: 73–157 ms longer

The results for the second experiment can be summarized as:

- reaction with discrimination, but no choice: 185–303 ms
- simple choice—152–184 ms longer
- multiple choice—188–331 ms longer

Wundt's experimental lab hosted hundreds of experiments utilizing various methods. Even from the initial experiments of the first doctoral students, problems had already arisen with some of Wundt's early theories. Tischer's dissertation on the discrimination of sounds, for instance, posed the already recognized situation that auditory stimulus involved a much shorter reaction time than visual. At times, the discrimination time appeared to be zero, with the time necessary to react to a sound stimulus the same as the time necessary to react when the stimulus was "recognized." Kraepelin revealed in his article, also in the first volume of *Philosophische Studien,* that discrimination time was particularly unreliable when the subject was influenced by drugs or alcohol. The American student Cattell, who had once been a devoted follower of Wundt, initially brought many improvements to the theory in his reaction-time experiments, only to abandon the pursuit later. His measurements lessened reaction times to such a degree that he was having a hard time keeping enough slack time to distinguish accurate discrimination time. Another student, Gustav

Berger, shared the distrust of the "d" reaction, deciding that there was no definitive method for determining false reactions or to say with certainty that an apperception has occurred.

Wundt's reaction-time experiments were met with great interest in the first decade of his lab. By the end of the second decade, however, that interest had begun to wane and the experiments were rare. The new trends started focusing on emotions, and behavior theorists began to multiply. But by 1905, as was evident by the publications in his second journal (then known as the *Psychologische Studien*), the reaction-time studies had become prominent again. Some of them featured the sensory reaction that used the subtraction method and incorporated Wundt's theory of emotions. As previously noted, Wundt's assistant at Leipzig, Wilhelm Wirth played a key role in bringing reaction-time studies back into focus.

Relevance to modern readers

Due to the complexity of Wundt's work, and the sheer magnitude of it, the impact that it has on twenty-first century humans might not be as quantifiable has Wundt himself would have liked. Reaction-time studies will certainly continue to shed the light on research into human performance. Rather than as Wundt used them, to test for his theories, modern psychologists are more likely to continue using them as a tool to understand human capabilities, or the challenges that face human potential.

Wundt did lay the groundwork for what modern psychologists do and how they practice their science. He has provided at least six generations of investigators into the human psyche with the solid basis for their existence. The question remains whether Wundt contributed anything more than historical value with regard to relevance for the modern student. One historian attempted to answer that question by commenting:

> prejudging the value of what history has led to always results in bad history. It also results in redundant history; for if the past merely represent imperfect stages along the path to the achievements of the present, why bother with it? But if we suspend judgment on whether the path taken by the majority was the right one or the wrong one, or more likely something in between, then the work of those who, like Wundt, took another path becomes much more interesting. For it is possible that it may open up perspectives that have been closed off by the biases of the present.

In fact, Wundt has provided all humans with a method by which to continue to examine themselves, and the state of their consciousness. In the early twenty-first century, the issue of dementia —usually appearing in the form of Alzheimer's disease—haunts medical and psychological research. Americans and other members of modern cultures throughout the world have a lifespan longer than any in the history of humankind; thus, the incidence of Alzheimer's disease is increasing rapidly. As researchers work furiously to uncover the mystery of a genetic link, those who work daily with those who have the disease face another issue: What sort of communication is possible as the patient retreats further into a vacant memory? Some research has begun to show that the sensations such as sound and touch, as well as visual stimuli of lights, can often spark some memory. A response such as the squeeze of a hand could give recognition to someone outside the patient's own confused mental state. Wundtian psychology represents the underlying strength than can motivate research in such areas as Alzheimer's, or even in studying the recovery from strokes or other "accidents" of the brain as well as other forms of mental illness.

Understanding Wundt's premise for glimpsing the human mind serves as a vital lesson. Opportunities for scientific discoveries must continually expand. No matter what the cause or reason, human sensations remain as relevant in the modern world as they did for Wundt in the laboratory. Wundt offers the experience that what *is* known about humans provides enough of a mystery for several lifetimes of research.

CHRONOLOGY

1832: Born in Neckarau, Baden, Germany, outside of Leipzig, on August 16.

1856: Receives a medical degree from the University of Heidelberg.

1857: Begins a seven-year position as lecturer in physiology at Heidelberg. During this time, serves as an assistant to renowned psychologist, physicist, and physiological psychologist Hermann von Helmholtz who arrived at Heidelberg in 1858.

1864: Appointed associate professor in physiology at University of Heidelberg.

1872: Marries Sophie Mau.

1873–74: Publishes first edition of *Principles of Psychology.*

1874: Appointed fellow professor of philosophy at Zurich University.

1875: Appointed one of two fellow professors at Leipzig University, focusing on practical-scientific theories.

1879: Establishes the laboratory for experimental psychology.

1883–84: Wundt's laboratory receives official status at Leipzig as an institution of its department of philosophy.

1896: Publishes *Outlines of Psychology.*

1900–20: Publishes *Volkerpsychologie (Folk Psychology).* 10 volumes.

1920: Publishes autobiography entitled *Erlebtes und Erkanntes.*

1896: Dies in Groábothen, German, near Leipzig, August 31.

BIBLIOGRAPHY

Sources

Allen, Gay Wilson. *William James.* New York: Viking Press, 1967.

American Psychological Society. *American Psychological Society* Web site. [cited April 2004.] http://www.psychologicalscience.org.

Boeree, C. George. *Wilhelm Wundt and William James.* Shippensburg, Pennsylvania: Shippensburg University, 1999, 2000. http://www.ship.edu/~cgboeree/wundtjames.html.

Feinstein, Howard M. *Becoming William James.* Ithaca and London: Cornell University Press, 1984.

"G. Stanley Hall." *PSI Cafe.* Psychology resource site, 2001. [cited April 2004] http://www.psy.pdx.edu/PsiCafe/KeyTheorists/Hall.]

James, William. *The Principles of Psychology.* Chicago: Encyclopedia Britannica, 1952.

James, William. "Psychology: Briefer Course." *Goethe, William James, Spinoza.* Set Five, Vol. 4. Chicago: Great Books Foundation, 1951; 1966; 1958; 2000.

James, William. *The Will to Believe, and Other Essays in Popular Philosophy.* Dover Publications, 1956.

James, William. *Writings 1902–1910, (The Varieties of Religious Experience, Pragmatism, A Pluralistic Universe, The Meaning of Truth, Some Problems of Philosophy, Essay).* New York: Literary Classics of the United States, 1987.

Meyers, Gerald. *William James, His Life and Thought.* New Haven and London: Yale University Press, 1986.

"Mind, Brain, and the Experimental Psychology of Consciousness." *Serendip.* Bryn Mawr College. September 3, 1996 [cited April 2004]. http://serendip.brynmawr.edu/exhibitions/Mind/Con

Ohles, John F., ed. *Biographical Dictionary of American Educators.* Vol. 2. Westport, CT: Greenwood Press, 1978.

Rieber, Robert W. and David K. Robinson, eds. *Wilhelm Wundt in History, The Making of a Scientific Psychology.* New York: Kluwer Academic/Plenum Publishers, 2001.

"Wilhelm Wundt." *Indiana University.* Dec. 11, 2003. http://www.indiana.edu/~intell/wundt.shtml.

"Wilhelm Wundt." *University of Leipzig (Germany).* [cited April 2004.] http://www.uni-leipzig.de/~psy/eng/Wundt-e.html.

"Wilhelm Wundt." *Lifschitz Psychology Museum.* Virtual Museum Web site. [cited April 2004.] http://www.netaxs.com/people/aca3/lpm-info.htm.

"Wilhelm Wundt." *McGraw-Hill/Dushkin.* 2004. http://www.dushkin.com/connectext/psy/ch01/wund

"Wilhelm Wundt." *PSI Cafe*. Psychology resource site, 2001. [cited April 2004.] http://www.psy.pdx.edu/PsiCafe/KeyTheorists/Wund

Sheehy, Noel, Antony J. Chapman, and Wendy A Conroy, eds. *Biographical Dictionary of Psychology*. London and New York: Routledge, 1997.

Washington, Peter. *Madame Blavatsky's Baboon: A History of the Mystics, Mediums, and Misfits Who Brought Spiritualism to America*. New York: Schocken Books, 1995.

Who Was Who in America. Vol. 1, 1897–1942, Chicago: A. N. Marquis Company, 1942.

Wundt, Wilhelm. *Principles of Physiological Psychology*. 1902. Translated by Edward Bradford Titchener, 1904.

Zusne, Leonard. *Biographical Dictionary of Psychology*. Westport, CT: Greenwood Press, 1984.